Unleash your potential

Unleash your potential: The groundbreaking approach you need to grow your business

BY

Jimmie V. Bond

TABLE OF CONTENT

INTRODUCTION

WHY YOU REQUIRE A SHOWCASING SYSTEM

What Is a Showcasing System?
A promoting procedure alludes to a business' general strategy for arriving at planned purchasers and transforming them into clients of their items or administrations. A showcasing technique contains the organization's incentive, key brand informing, information on track client socioeconomics, and other significant level components.

An intensive showcasing technique covers the four Ps of advertising: item, value, spot, and advancement.

KEY FOCUS POINTS
A showcasing technique is a business' strategy for arriving at imminent buyers and

transforming them into clients of their items or administrations. Promoting techniques ought to spin around an organization's incentive.

A definitive objective of a showcasing system is to accomplish and convey a practical upper hand over rival organizations.

Grasping Promoting Methodologies

An unmistakable showcasing procedure ought to rotate around the organization's offer, which conveys to customers what the organization relies on, how it works, and why it merits their business. This gives showcasing groups a layout that ought to educate their drives across all regarding the organization's items and administrations. For instance, Walmart (WMT) is commonly known as a markdown retailer with "ordinary low costs," whose business tasks and promoting endeavors are established in that thought.

This furnishes showcasing groups with a format that ought to illuminate their drives across all regarding the organization's

items and administrations. For instance, Walmart (WMT) is commonly known as a rebate retailer with "regular low costs," whose business tasks and **showcasing endeavors are established in that thought.**
Showcasing Techniques versus Showcasing Plans
The promotion procedure is illustrated in the showcasing plan —a report that details the particular sorts of advertising exercises that an organization leads and contains schedules for carrying out different showcasing drives.

Promoting systems ought to in a perfect world have longer life expectancies than individual showcasing plans since they contain incentives and other key components of an organization's image, which by and large hold steady over an extended time. All in all, advertising systems cover higher perspective informing, while at the same time promoting plans outline the strategic subtleties of explicit missions.

Advantages of a Showcasing System

A definitive objective of a showcasing system is to accomplish and convey a practical upper hand over rival organizations by grasping the necessities and needs of its purchasers. Whether it's a print promotion configuration, mass customization, or a web-based entertainment crusade, a showcasing resource can be passed judgment on in light of how it really conveys an organization's guiding principle recommendation.

Statistical surveying can assist with graphing the viability of a given mission and can assist with recognizing undiscovered crowds to accomplish main concern objectives and increment deals

Instructions to Come up with a Promoting Procedure

Thinking up a promoting methodology requires a couple of steps. HubSpot, a computerized promoting asset, offers knowledge into how to formulate your system.

Fete your objects While deals are a definitive ideal for each association, you ought to have all the more flash objects, for illustration, laying out power, expanding customer commitment, or creating leads. These more modest objects offer quantifiable marks for the advancement of your promoting plan. Consider fashion, the significant position gospel and arranging as how you achieve your objects. Know your guests Each item or administration has an optimal customer, and you ought to know what their identity is and where they hang out. Assuming you vend power accouterments , you will pick promoting channels where general design workers might see your information. Lay out who your customer is and the way that your item will work on their lives. Make your communication Now that you know your objects and who you are pitching to, now is the ideal time to make your information. This is your chance to show your implicit guests how your item or administration will help them and for what reason you're the main organization that can give it.

Characterize your spending plan: How you scatter your

information might rely on the amount you can manage. Will you be buying and promoting? Expecting a viral second via online entertainment naturally? Conveying public statements to the media to attempt to acquire inclusion? Your spending plan will direct what you can bear to do.

Decide your channels: Even the best message needs the suitable setting. A few organizations might track down more worth in making blog entries for their site. Others might make progress with paid advertisements via online entertainment channels. Track down the most proper scene for your substance.

Measure your prosperity: To focus on your advertising, you really want to understand whether it is arriving at its listeners' perspective. Decide your measurements and how you'll pass judgment on the outcome of your showcasing endeavors

For what reason does my organization require a promotion procedure?

A promoting methodology assists an organization with guiding its publicizing dollars to where it will have the most effect. Contrasted and the information from 2018, the relationship among association and outcome in advertisers hopped from being very nearly multiple times bound to right multiple times more probable in 2022

These are the key factors that are engaged with the showcasing of a decent or administration. The four Ps can be utilized while arranging another undertaking, assessing a current deal, or attempting to enhance deals with a main interest group. It likewise can be utilized to test an ongoing showcasing methodology on another crowd.

What does a showcasing technique resemble?

A showcasing system will detail the promoting, effort, and advertising efforts to be done by a firm, including how the organization will gauge the impact of these drives. They will commonly follow the four Ps. The capabilities and parts of a showcasing plan incorporate statistical surveying to help estimating choices and new market sections, custom-made informing that objectives certain socioeconomics and geographic regions, and stage determination for item and administration advancement — computerized, radio, web, exchange magazines, and the blend of those stages for each mission, and measurements that action the consequences of promoting endeavors and their revealing courses of events.

Is a showcasing system equivalent to a promoting plan?

The expressions "promoting plan" and "showcasing technique" are frequently utilized reciprocally in light of the fact that a promoting plan is created in view of a general key structure. At times, the methodology and the arrangement might be integrated into one report, especially for more modest organizations that may just run a couple of significant missions in a year. The arrangement frames promoting exercises on a month to month, quarterly, or yearly premise, while the showcasing methodology frames the general offer.

CHAPTER 1:

SELECTING YOUR TARGET MARKET

An objective market is the particular gathering you need to reach with your showcasing message. They are individuals who are probably going to purchase your items or administrations, and they are joined by a few normal qualities, similar to socioeconomics and ways of behaving.

The more plainly you characterize your objective market, the better you can grasp how and where to arrive at your optimal expected clients. You can begin with general classifications like millennial or single parents, however you really want to get substantially more definite than that to accomplish the most ideal transformation rates.

Make it a point to get profoundly unambiguous. This is tied in with focusing on your advertising endeavors actually, not preventing individuals from purchasing your item.

Individuals who are excluded from your designated advertising can in any case purchase from your they're simply not your top center while making your showcasing system. You can't target everybody, except you can offer to everybody.

Your objective market ought to be founded on research, not a premonition. You really want to pursue individuals who truly need to purchase from you, regardless of whether they're not the clients you initially set off to reach.

What is target market division?

Target market division is the most common way of separating your objective market into more modest, more unambiguous gatherings.

It permits you to make a more important promoting message for each gathering.

Recall — you can't be everything to all individuals. Be that as it may, you can be various things to various gatherings.

For instance, as a veggie lover, I've eaten a lot of Inconceivable Burgers. I'm certainly an objective client. Be that as it may, veggie lovers are a shockingly little objective market fragment for

Incomprehensible Food varieties: just 10% of their client base.

The objective market portion for this promotion crusade was "meat eaters who haven't yet attempted Unthinkable products."Vegetarians and meat eaters have various explanations behind eating plant-based burgers and need various things from the experience. Target market division guarantees the organization contacts the right crowd with the right message.

Instructions to characterize your objective market

1.Compile information on your ongoing clients

An extraordinary initial phase in sorting out who most needs to purchase from you is to distinguish who is as of now utilizing your items or administrations. When you comprehend the central attributes of your current client base, you can pursue more individuals like that.

Contingent upon how somebody interfaces with your business, you could have just a little data about them, or a great deal

This doesn't mean you ought to add a ton of inquiries to your request or select in process only for crowd research purposes — this can pester clients and result in deserted shopping baskets.

Be that as it may, do make certain to utilize the data you normally gain to figure out patterns and midpoints.

A few information focuses you should consider are:

Age: You don't have to get excessively unambiguous here. It won't probably have an effect whether your typical client is 24 or 27. However, knowing which ten years of life your clients are in can be exceptionally valuable.

Area (and time region): Where on earth do your current clients reside? As well as understanding which geographic regions to focus on, this assists you with sorting out what hours are generally significant for your client care and agents to be on the web, and what time you ought to plan your

social advertisements and presents guarantee best perceivability.

Language: Don't accept your clients communicating in a similar language as you do. Also, don't expect them to communicate in the predominant language of their (or your) current actual area.

Spending influence and examples: How much cash do your ongoing clients need to spend? How would they move toward buys in your cost class?

Interests: What do your clients get a kick out of the chance to do, other than utilizing your items or administrations? What Television programs do they watch? What different organizations do they connect with?

Challenges: What trouble spots are your clients confronting? Do you comprehend how your item or administration assists them with tending to those difficulties? Phase of life: Are your clients prone to be understudies? Unseasoned parents? Guardians of teenagers? Retired folks

2. Consolidate social information.

Virtual entertainment examination can be an incredible approach to finishing up the image of your objective market. They assist you with figuring out who's collaborating with your social records, regardless of whether those individuals are not yet clients.

These individuals are keen on your image. Social investigation can give a great deal of data that could end up being useful to you to figure out why. You'll likewise find out about potential market portions you might not have remembered to focus on previously.

You can likewise utilize social standing by listening to assist with recognizing individuals who are discussing you and your item via web-based entertainment, regardless of whether they follow you. To arrive at your objective market with social advertisements, carbon copy crowds are a simple method for contacting more individuals who share qualities with your best clients.

3. Checkout the opposition.

Since it is now so obvious who's now communicating with your business and purchasing your items or administrations, now is the ideal time to see who's drawing in with the opposition.

Understanding what your rivals are doing can assist you with addressing a few key inquiries:

Are your rivals pursuing similar objective market fragments as you are?

Is it true or not that they are arriving at fragments you hadn't remembered to consider?

How can they situate themselves?

You will not have the option to get definite crowd data about individuals connecting with your rivals, yet you'll have the option to get a general feeling of the methodology they're taking and whether it's permitting them to make a commitment on the web.

This examination will assist you with understanding which market contenders are focusing on and whether their endeavors seem, by all accounts, to be powerful for those sections.

4. Explain the worth of your item or administration.

This boils down to the key differentiation all advertisers should comprehend among highlights and advantages. You can list the elements of your item the entire day, yet nobody will be persuaded to purchase from you except if you can make sense of the advantages.

Your item is or does highlight. The advantages are the outcomes. How does your item make somebody's life simpler, or better, or really intriguing?

On the off chance that you don't as of now have an unmistakable rundown of the advantages of your item, now is the ideal time to begin conceptualizing now. As you make your advantage articulations, you'll likewise as a matter of course be expressing some fundamental data about your main interest group.

For instance, assuming your administration assists individuals with tracking down somebody to take care of their pets while they're away, you can be quite sure that your market will have two principal fragments:
(1) animal people and
(2) existing or expected pet-sitters.
On the off chance that you don't know precisely the way in which clients benefit from utilizing your items, why not ask them in an overview, or even a virtual entertainment survey? You could find that individuals utilize your items or administrations for purposes you haven't even considered. That may, thus, change how you see your objective market for future deals.

5. Make an objective market proclamation

Presently it is the ideal time to bubble all that you've found such a long way into one straightforward proclamation that characterizes your objective market. This is really the most vital phase in making a brand situating explanation, however that is an undertaking for one more day.

CHAPTER 2:

MASTERING YOUR MARKET STRATEGY

With regards to your business and where you desire to go in the following year, this moment is the best opportunity for some reflection. Carve out some margin for yourself before very long to sit back, unwind, and really investigate how your year went, how you might have veered off-track, and the numerous manners by which you can get doing great.

If, as so many, you have attempted to accomplish your showcasing, the following are a couple of tips for how to take care of business.

Put resources into your site

Rome wasn't implicit a day, nor was that marvelous site. Assuming you have been battling to track down the ideal site for your business, realize that you are in good company. A classy, useful site is in no way, shape or form simple to drop by. It could require months or years before you at last raise yours to an acceptable level.

Regardless of whether you've poured your entire being (and hard-brought in cash) into your business site, there are many motivations behind why it might in any case, notwithstanding your earnest attempts, get ugly. There's even an opportunity that your ongoing site isn't doing a lot of by any stretch of the imagination concerning new deals. From an absence of usefulness to message weighty locales that can straight-up exhaust a man, there is bounty that can turn out badly with a site, regardless of how much cash you toss at it. Put resources into a practical site through a trustworthy web improvement expert and you'll perceive the way a lot more straightforward maintaining your business can be.

Plan your substance

Content is a blade that cuts both ways. It very well may be sufficiently troublesome to make great, important substance, yet even after that — you've actually got to post the stuff. That is where booking comes in.

Why require a month to do what should be possible in a day? An excessive number of entrepreneurs battle with what and when to post to virtual entertainment when that time can be better spent on working said business. Saving a couple of days of the month to make content and planning your virtual entertainment posts through outsider programming like Meet Edgar or Later can make the possibility of a reliable online entertainment presence substantially more feasible.

Think about a coordinated effort

Allow us to introduce this by saying joint efforts won't work for everybody. While Adweek has recorded brand-to-mark coordinated efforts as one of the top showcasing patterns for 2021, it's conceivable your plan of action simply doesn't take into consideration such a procedure. Also, that is Completely fine.

In any case, in the event that it's a good idea for your business, a breathtaking cooperation might be exactly what you want to reinvigorate your showcasing endeavors. Whether a cooperative Instagram giveaway, an exceptional Purchase 1, Get one advancement, or a straightforward reference code, consider how joint efforts can assist you with fortifying your promotion from now into the foreseeable future.

Assess your account

What is your story? What are your qualities? When others consider your business and brand, what do they see? Could it be said that you are known for your great client support? Your novel menu? Your executioner's hard working attitude?

The year's end is a great opportunity to ponder your image and how it affects you. Do your site and online entertainment channels obviously convey what your identity is and why you do what you do?

On the off chance that not, you have some spirit looking to do. Assess your account and change it until it seems like… you. Whether that implies a snappy new trademark, a complete rebrand, or something as basic as additional lively virtual entertainment content, take some real time to contemplate what your image addresses and alter your promoting materials to mirror this.

Grow your land

No, we don't mean purchase more houses, however couldn't unreasonably be great? By land, we mean web land. This implies getting your image out there. Truly something else.

Extending your web land implies enlisting your business with registries, survey applications, and such. On the off chance that you own a physical retail facade and your items are not accessible to buy on the web — same difference either way. Growing your internet based land implies expanding the possibilities of your image getting seen across the web. In the event that you don't have a strong web-based presence, you are harming your image and now is the ideal time to take care of business.

Keep it genuine

There's a typical confusion that the less you discuss something, the less it is observable. This may be valid while, say… passing gas, however it unquestionably doesn't matter to all in that frame of mind of Coronavirus. The Covid pandemic is at the forefront of everybody's thoughts, and no measure of moving around the subject will make this less so. Rather than hiding hard points away from view, think about a cautious way to deal with putting it out in the open. We guarantee your crowd will regard you for it. Civil rights is top-of-mind for some shoppers, and information shows they need to hear from the organizations from which they purchase. This implies featuring your organization's way of life, your position on significant social issues, and your arrangements for how to make the world a superior spot. On the off chance that you don't have an arrangement, there could be no greater opportunity to make one. The sooner you do, the sooner you'll see an effect.

Redesign the client experience

Client experience is significant, yet you might be underrating exactly the way that significant it is. While factors like cost once directed where clients decide to shop, client experience is presently the determinant. From a showcasing outlook, you maintain that your client's involvement in your image should be first class beginning to end.

The most vital phase in raising the client experience is tending to their requirements at every turn. Is your site simple to explore?

Does it have a FAQ segment to rapidly and effectively address normal client questions?

Might it be said that you are fast to answer when they shoot you a FB message in passing?

When your client ventures into your store, would they say they are welcomed happily or overlooked?

How simple is it for them to buy your item or administration?

Then, they're doing an amazing job for your client's insight. Assuming you're an independent company, you could find that written by hand notes included with transported merchandise can be compelling. Customizing your client experience can go far in building reliability, which can possibly take your business places you never imagined.

Try not to excuse advanced advertisements

Aimlessly tossing cash at your promotion spending plan doesn't function as well as it used to. In a terrible economy, each dollar counts. For this reason you need to painstakingly consider your promotion procedure and whether your cash is being put toward the most ideal use. Chances are, it's not.

Building a promotion methodology that seems OK for your business could include a few hard choices. With the progress of computerized promotions at a record-breaking high, it very well might be an ideal opportunity to roll out improvements concerning how your promotion dollars are spent.

Rather than burning through many dollars on the odd nearby magazine or radio spot, ponder how far those many dollars can go online where your crowd is.

Construct your local area

Everybody needs more likes, more remarks, more adherents. In any case, how? The most important phase in the situation is to free yourself of the thought that your web-based entertainment needs a huge number of supporters to find success. Nowadays, that simply isn't accurate.

Do whatever it takes not to zero in so vigorously on vanity measurements. Huge number of supporters might appear to be engaging and send you the mixed signal you're doing everything right, except this could be a long way from the real world. All things considered — how kindly many devotees help you assuming that not a solitary one of them are ready to purchase in fact?

What is significant, however, is that your devotees are the right sort of supporters — the individuals who will communicate with your business on a more profound level. Put some work into teaching and engaging your crowd and further developing their lives the way you can. This can be with tips connected with your industry, or fun realities and random data. Consider new ideas and come at the situation from your optimal client's perspective to explore the errand of building your commitment. What might you need to see? Begin there.

Create the ideal source of inspiration

Numerous organizations work really hard to put out the right information. One thing frequently missing is the ideal source of inspiration to back it up.

For what reason is a source of inspiration significant?

A source of inspiration is probably the last thing your peruser will see when they run over your business via virtual entertainment at some random time. Without a reasonable and brief source of inspiration that explains to them why and how to buy your great or administration, you may not be extending your substance to the extent that it can go. This is not to indicate that that all of your substance ought to have a source of alleviation. All effects considered, nothing needs to be continually offered to. Vast suggestions to take action can appear disingenuine and, in all honesty, frantic. In any case, know that the ideal source of alleviation has the capability to change over your crowd into guests — a definitive ideal of your motorized presence. Primary concern do not pass on your suggestions to take action up

CHAPTER 3:

WHO ARE YOUR CUSTOMERS

Fruitful associations truly figure out their guests. Knowing your interest group is a portion of the fight with respect to fostering a fruitful charge. Likewise, when you comprehend the particular rates and musts of your customer base, you can convey your answer at the right cost, impeccably deposited and in their language. More deeply study your guests and you'll be in front of your opposition in a matter of seconds. This will set away your time and cash over the long haul. It's tied in with going gradually now to go fleetly later. By responding to the accompanying inquiries, you'll actually want to both distinguish and open the capability of your guests. What kind of customer do you need? The kind of customer you need for your business depends by and large on the kind of business you're running and the business it works in. For case, a business dealing particulars with an extravagant cost point easily needs to intrigue guests with better than anticipated hires. A mass-request retail business, also again, requests an alternate arrangement of guests. To decide the kind of customer you need for your business, first break down the business you work in and the attributes of the common purchasers of particulars like those your association sells. In doing as similar, suppose about the coexisting rates Their socioeconomics Age coitus Identity Pay situations Geographic area Whenever you've instanced the guests you need to draw in, presently break down the different purchasing ways of carrying and figure out which are presumably going to be the most important to your business. One- off purchasers Semi Ceaseless purchasers Incessant purchasers Do guests convey further worth to your business than others? In 1906 Vilfredo Pareto cooked the' 80/20' rule. The standard recommends that the top 20 of your guests address 80 or your income. These are presumably going to be the customer base you'll need to zero in on.

What income do you believe that they should bring?

Extending income from your ideal client assists pressure with testing your strategy. All things considered, promotion isn't free, when in doubt, it demands both investment and cash.

Do you have any idea how much income every client brings to your business? This makes it a lot simpler to conclude the amount you ought to spend in gaining those clients.

To sort out your return for capital invested, take a gander at the costs engaged with securing every client far in excess of above costs. You might be spending excessively or maybe it will show you that you can legitimize an expansion in your promoting financial plan.

Understanding your client and the job your item plays in their lives

Promoting is simpler when you have a decent comprehension of precisely who your clients are and the way that your item addresses their issues. Understanding the socioeconomics for your common clients is significant, however it likewise seems OK to perform subjective, as well as quantitative investigation into their qualities.

Grasp Your Ongoing Clients - Take a gander at the clients and clients that are generally significant to you. Are there normal qualities?

Use Overviews and Surveys - request criticism on how clients utilize your item or what benefits they search for and esteem

Take a gander at Remarks or Regularly Clarify some pressing issues - Are there normal issues that you resolve for them?

Utilize Web-based Entertainment - The intuitive idea of virtual entertainment enables you to draw in with individuals and fabricate an image of your clients.

Understanding the job your item plays in their day to day existence is significant as well. Furthermore, this might change with time. You could portion your clients in light of this:

Easygoing client: These purchasers utilize an item at times, yet it doesn't assume a significant part in their lives nor do they really think about to its buy.

Spurred client: Purchasers of this kind are exceptionally energetic to consume your item and think of it as a huge figure in their lives. Subsequently, they will frequently do broad examination into an item prior to making a buy.

Way of life centered client: These clients partner your item with the way of life they lead or might want to lead. Item and brand picture are vital to clients of this sort.

How would you contact them - What channels would they say they are utilizing consistently?

Knowing your clients' qualities and attributes is valuable with regards to concocting a promoting effort to contact them. Different segment bunches will more often than not favor various kinds of media, so definite information on your client base will assist you in conceiving a promotion with battling to contact them.

Generational gatherings have various media utilization propensities. For instance:

Gen X-ers: This gathering will in general consume customary media sources, for example, television, radio and written word like papers and magazines for news and data. While some utilize online entertainment, it isn't normally their essential media source for all intents and purposes for some twenty to thirty year olds. Thus, a mission to arrive at this gathering may not be as virtual entertainment engaged as one designated at a more youthful age. Conventional media showcasing sources ought to be considered as well as less intelligent web based promoting approaches, for example, email promoting, which can contact this crowd at a lower cost than utilizing customary media.

Recent college grads: Collectively, twenty to thirty year olds are substantially more liable to involve different types of virtual entertainment as their primary wellspring of media utilization. A portion of this gathering has even "cut the string," abandoning the utilization of conventional media and just consuming media conveyed on the web. This gathering can be reached through a web-based entertainment weighty promoting effort that utilizes pretty much nothing on the off chance that any customary media sources.

Age X: This gathering falls between the children of post war America and the recent college grads both sequentially and as far as their media utilization propensities. They keep a foot in the two camps, so your missions with components from both conventional media and virtual entertainment can have accomplishment with them.

How would you secure them as clients?

Your clients might contact you in various ways. Natural obtaining incorporates savvy ways of changing over outsiders into clients. It may very well be by means of verbal, web-based entertainment outreach or inbound promoting strategies, for example, a connection with a blog entry that stands out and situates you well when they are prepared to purchase.

Natural procurement procedures are a fundamental component of your advertising. Individuals that you are focusing on track down you through your websites, web crawlers and virtual entertainment. This implies they are 'qualified' and the work you do on your messages and content assists with building validity and trust. That's what the other side is and keeping in mind that these methods are 'neglected' they can consume time and take more time to prove to be fruitful.

Your showcasing objectives will figure out what approach you take for crusades.

Think about the accompanying variables:

Crusade plan: On the off chance that your mission is intended to accomplish quick outcomes, paying for leads might be the best methodology. Natural strategies, for example, satisfied promoting, building an email mailing rundown and virtual entertainment effort can give strong outcomes over the long haul, however these techniques regularly require months or even a long time to have a huge effect. Subsequently, for fast outcomes either utilizing paid showcasing endeavors, for example, web search tool promoting (SEM), buying email mailing records or customary publicizing endeavors by means of television, print advertisements or radio alone or in mix with natural endeavors is probably going to be the best methodology.

Crusade financial plan: In the event that your promoting spending plan is restricted, natural effort endeavors are an extraordinary choice and ought to shape the foundation of your showcasing action. Doing so permits you to utilize paid promoting endeavors decisively where they are generally required while as yet chasing after natural endeavors consistently.

Significant crowd: In the event that your client base is now conveying through virtual entertainment, your natural strategies will arrive at a greater amount of them. Recent college grads particularly are probably going to impart great encounters to items or brands on the web and the verbal exchange is enhanced when it's common and enjoyed. Find the stages that are the most ideal to your crowd to get the news out about your items.

Knowing and understanding your clients is critical to fruitful business and can give you a beneficial benefit. You can fit your item or administration to their requirements, be more convincing in your promotion and furthermore make a more sure purchasing experience. Find opportunity to comprehend your esteemed clients and you'll be bound to prevail with regards to drawing in more.

The most effective method to get to know your clients

Getting to know clients and understanding their inspirations for buying items or administrations can assist organizations with creating solid advertising methodologies and increment their general deals and income. Assuming you're expecting to interface more with customers, it's essential to comprehend the most effective ways to impart and draw in with them. In this article, we examine the reason why it's essential to draw in with clients and give a rundown of moves toward assisting you with setting to realize your clients better to successfully further develop your showcasing efforts.

For what reason is it vital to know your clients?

Getting to realize your clients is significant on the grounds that it can assist you with grasping a shopper's buying choices. This can assist you with expanding the adequacy of your promoting efforts by focusing on clients with one of a kind and compelling publicizing systems that urge them to purchase your labor and products. For instance, assuming you realize that a large number of your clients utilize specific online entertainment stages, it very well may be valuable to utilize those stages to publicize your business and brand.

Instructions to know your clients

Here is a rundown of steps you can use to all the more likely grasp your clients:

1. Converse with clients

Conversing with clients is quite possibly the simplest step you can take to get to realize them better. While bantering with them, it may very well be useful to ask them inquiries that give you accommodating knowledge into their buying choices and perspectives about the organization. This can assist you with serving them better and make it simpler to explain any inquiries they could have about your image and the administrations you offer. Assuming a client is confused about your items or administrations, that may be a marker to change your correspondence or promoting procedures.

2. Direct reviews

Directing studies is an incredible method for understanding your clients better since it can give you supportive input on the advantages of your items, and it permits you to comprehend the buying system according to the client's perspective. While making studies, consider posing inquiries that clients can respond to rapidly to assist with empowering them to take the overview and furnish you with their input. **Those questions can include:**

- How does the item address your issues?
- Is there anything you feel is missing?
- What issues would you say you are trusting our item can tackle?
- How might you rate the buying system?
- Could it be said that you were ready to find the data you really wanted?
- Did our group respond to your inquiries really?

3. Audit information

On the off chance that you're selling your items or administrations on the web, you could approach powerful information from outsider programming that can assist you with deciding significant buyer factors, like age, orientation and area. Moreover, this information might assist you with finding your organization's purchaser-to-guest proportion, which can perceive you the number of site guests wound up making a buy. This data can assist you with understanding the sort of clients you're drawing into the business and conclude whether you really want to change your promoting methodologies. This can help you all the more effectively characterize your objective shopper and increment your general deals and income.

4. Make client profiles

Making client profiles from supportive information can permit you to fit your publicizing to specific customers and come up with compelling showcasing procedures. Client profiles can assist organizations with understanding their objective client's age, occupation and other supportive publicizing data. They can likewise list a couple of potential difficulties or issues that a client may be confronting and the way in which the business' items can best serve them. This can permit organizations to comprehend which promoting efforts could draw in the most measure of clients.

For instance, assuming an organization realizes that a greater part of its clients are suburbanites, a radio or web recording notice may be a viable showcasing procedure.

5. Hold occasions

Holding occasions in neighborhoods assists with giving an open door to you to collaborate with your clients and make a vital encounter for them. This can assist with expanding client faithfulness and effort as you illuminate clients more about your image and the labor and products you offer. For instance, on the off chance that an organization sells various sorts of sweets, a free tasting occasion could urge new clients to attempt their items.

Be that as it may, assuming your organization directs a ton of business on the web, it very well may be more valuable to hold virtual occasions to interface with clients. If so, consider utilizing online classes or live transmissions to speak with shoppers or deal them a tomfoolery game they can play and connect with practically.

6. Use catchphrase research

Catchphrase examination can permit organizations to find what people are looking for in regards to their organization or items. With this data, organizations can all the more likely comprehend how clients communicate with their business and straightforwardly address any normal different kinds of feedback people have about their administrations. For instance, assuming an organization that sells clothing found that a ton of clients were utilizing web indexes to inquire as to whether the garments were irritated, they could utilize that data to address the texture they make their dress with or make notices that educated purchasers about their attire's smooth and agreeable materials.

7. Put resources into content advertising

Content showcasing is a compelling method for giving helpful data to an organization's clients while at the same time advancing their items or administrations. This promoting style frequently includes utilizing content, like articles, web journals, recordings and the sky's the limit from there, to productively speak with clients and answer their inquiries. While making a substance promoting effort, attempt to utilize catchphrases to focus on specific themes that a larger part of clients are examining or getting some information about. This can permit you to answer those points and obviously lay out your organization's image while expanding consumer loyalty and steadfastness.

8. Follow client surveys

Following client audits can be significant in light of the fact that they frequently furnish organizations and associations with powerful criticism. This can assist organizations with understanding assuming that they need to make vital acclimations to their cycle to increment consumer loyalty. For instance, in the event that various clients leave negative surveys about an item since it broke too effectively, it may very well be beneficial for an organization to look at the material they use to develop their items.

It can likewise be useful to answer audits whenever the situation allows. Whether the survey is positive or negative, answering the client and either expressing gratitude toward them for their buy or inquisitive about their terrible experience can assist with acculturating the business collaboration and assist the organization with exhibiting how they care about their purchasers.

9. Utilize online entertainment

Making an online entertainment page or record can permit organizations to communicate more with clients. This is on the grounds that virtual entertainment offers clients the chance to contact organizations and organizations straightforwardly to ask them inquiries about their items or administrations. It additionally permits organizations to speak with clients who post surveys or remarks about the business. This can exhibit that the organization is dynamic in its shopper commitment and able to offer help, which can frequently assist with expanding consumer loyalty and dedication.

10. Research contenders

By investigating contenders, organizations can find new promoting procedures that different organizations see as fruitful, which can furnish them with instructive showcasing information to assist them with communicating with clients all the more proficiently. It can likewise show them famous items or administrations clients are buying that they don't at present give. This can assist organizations with growing new items that purchasers need or need, which can increment consumer loyalty and income.

11. Focus on your deals

Focusing on unambiguous buyers or furnishing them with fitted advancements can assist with spurring them to buy your items and administrations. This is on the grounds that customized deals can cause clients to feel like they're getting an exceptional advancement coordinated explicitly to them. While creating special strategies and promoting efforts, consider conveying purchasing impetuses to people who pursue your email list or your organization participation program. This can assist them with feeling like they're being compensated for drawing in with the organization and urge them to make a buy

CHAPTER 4:

WHAT DO THEY WANT

Client needs are those needs that drive and rouse a client to pick and buy an item or administration. The need can be anything that drives them to arrive at an answer. Any rationale that makes a client purchase an item is a driver in their choice. This need is a chance to give worth to clients in return for financial or unwaveringly esteem.

For any new entrepreneur or business person, achievement is vital. There are a few measuring sticks across which it is estimated. One of them is how much clients need to progress, purchase the item or administration, and keep utilizing it.

To accomplish this, it is important to get a comprehension of how clients act, the market, socioeconomics, selling factors, and in particular purchaser needs and persona.

Recognizing client needs is the most proficient method for supporting the exhibition of any brand. Each thought should be approved by clients. In the event that thoughts are not working, it could be something that matches client needs. An imperative piece of the development of any business is consumer loyalty. To fulfill clients, it is critical to realize client needs.

There are numerous ways of distinguishing client needs. It is feasible to recognize client needs from various sources like-

- Current clients
- Previous clients
- Online gatherings
- Your self
- Representatives

Consider Client Conduct

It is vital to think about client conduct to comprehend assuming that they make them need. When

you recognize angles you need to think about, it assists framing relationships with the item. Posing significant inquiries like-

- Inspirations
- Accessible choices
- Objectives or targets

At the point when you remember client conduct, understanding their needs is simple.

Notice conduct

Reflect and see your own way of behaving. What are a few viewpoints that you feel can change? What are the choices ahead to pick an item? Likewise, leave there are any activities or remunerating ways of behaving when an item or administration isn't up to the full assumptions for the clients. Does it satisfy client needs totally?

Construct perceptions

With the data from the previous, it is important to assemble perceptions and find out about the dynamic interaction from that. These experiences can be helpful in featuring open, areas of strength for doors, dangers, and issues if any. It is additionally simple to investigate how purchasers pick their items starting here.

Cost

Clients' esteem stickers cost a great deal. On the off chance that they feel the item is evaluated way higher than the normal, or contenders, they won't favor it. On the off chance that there is quality in the item or not, clients will consider. Almost 60% of clients feel that cost is the main thing they consider prior to purchasing anything more.

In the event that items are comparative or exceptional, chances of cost being a game changer are more. Offering limits, promotion codes, and different proposals on item packages will help gigantically. These motions will go far in addressing client needs and keeping up with faithfulness.

Usefulness and accommodation

Don't we as a whole cherish items that are not difficult to utilize, explore across, and work with? For any item to address client issues, it should be advantageous and valuable. There should be a degree of usefulness engaged with items.

At the point when you distinguish client needs, cutting items around it is better. This will likewise help adjust to client needs in a superior way.

Most organizations continue to deliver variants of their items to comprehend what highlights and angles fit the client 's needs. Take for instance, SmartKarrot's item reception included. It assists organizations with understanding how each element is performing. That improves and sharpens these elements for better maintenance.

Unwavering quality and Manageability

The help or item an organization is attempting to sell should be dependable, supportable, and advantageous. These are essential to work in a way any client will cherish. Clients need to depend on an item to become faithful clients. One part of this is bringing out solid, superior grade, supportable items that are helpful.

Assuming your item use is excessively complicated for utilization, chances of clients utilizing, or understanding are less. Subsequently, it is expected to ensure the item is all around refreshed and promoted according to client needs.

Risk decrease

Regardless of how great your items are, on the off chance that clients see them as dangerous, they won't turn up. Your items should be dependable, productive, and reliable. Having a straightforward merchandise exchange, free preliminary or ensures will assist with lessening risk vigorously. A significant variable to think about in order to decrease risk for clients is having a straightforward strategy. Quieting clients' fears will show them that they are not in a flawed, dangerous organization. The item should be tried from a security point generally.

Sympathy

Clients love brands and clients who care about them. Actually, in excess of 50% of individuals who experience terrible client assistance always avoid the organization. This implies a decent client experience is what clients need. Client needs include those items or administrations that are sympathetic to their prerequisites.

Experience

For clients to utilize your item, they should be clear, succinct, and all around put. Clients need to have the experience to successfully utilize the items. In the event that the clients are new to the field, they probably won't grasp the degree of intricacy of the organization contributions.

Plan

The UX configuration is everything. In the event that a client deals with an issue scrounging through the site or client page, it should be arranged. For clients to have the inspiration to hold with the organization or carry on with work in any case, the UX configuration should be first rate.

Effectiveness

Imagine a scenario in which the item and the client are not in total agreement. The item/administration should be smoothed out for the client to ensure the cycle isn't tedious.

Execution

Clients search for execution. The help or item should be on top execution so clients can accomplish their objectives. Clients will pick items that are high performing.

Straightforwardness

The organization should be pretty much as straightforward as conceivable with clients. Clients merit a receptiveness concerning the business regarding item, administration, evaluating, and that's just the beginning.

Risk

Assuming there are any dangers implied in partnering with an organization, that should be represented. In the event that a client needs conveyance protection, they need to know about the dangers implied.

Terms

Clients additionally expect that they coordinate with the organization in specific terms of administration. For example, terms like security, GDPR, and more should be maintained in the center. Clients are propelled by comparative terms. In the event that there are lesser legitimate entanglements in progress, they would be more keen on banding together.

Reconciliations and Similarity
Clients additionally incline toward brands where administrations and items work with different items or administrations. The combinations should be viable with their prerequisites. For instance assuming that a client is utilizing a specific joining, they would like to have an accomplice utilizing or fit for giving in that reconciliation. Similarity in innovation is likewise something clients need.

Data

Clients having the right data will be useful in making any buy or affiliation. Organizations need to offer clients instructive substance, recordings, and examination that will assist them with effectively utilizing the item or administration. Client needs are met exclusively through data.

Control

Clients favor simpler returns, memberships, terms and more. At the point when they feel like they are in charge of the organization, they will feel calm with regards to activity.

Assortment of Choices

Clients need different choices in item, membership, administrations, correspondence, and installments. Clients having that opportunity of decision causes them to feel significant and esteemed.

Openness

Clients expect that they should get to help and administration groups of the other firm. This implies multi-channel correspondence experience. At the point when organizations are more open, chances of them satisfying client needs are more.

What is a Client Needs Investigation?

A client needs investigation is one that gives a profound examination into client conduct to ensure that client necessities coordinate with item advantages or needs. It fosters the brand and item better and deal the client's better worth. To do a client's investigation, here are the accompanying advances.

Client Needs Study

A client's examination flourishes with client studies. These reviews will assist organizations comprehend their situation

concerning client needs. The review needs to incorporate inquiries connecting with
- Item mindfulness
- Brand inclinations
- Contenders
- Why-What Examination

When you comprehend the review, you really want to sort out why a client would purchase your item and what that would be. You can then channel the can choices as-
- Highlights
- Benefits
- Uniqueness

What are the highlights? What advantages are being advertised? Is the item remarkably addressing an issue?

Client Criticism

To investigate clients to satisfy client needs better, you want to take client input. Talking with clients who have worked effortlessly out any marks of contact. You will comprehend what to improve, construct, and change.h

Understanding client needs will help organizations modify and tailor advertising, deals, and client commitment. Knowing the requirements of clients will influence item advancement, research, client care, and that's only the tip of the iceberg.

The most effective way to understand what clients need is to ask them. A portion of the things you hear could shock you. The principal question will be, would you say you will carry out the thoughts your best clients give? We should investigate a portion of the criticism you might hear:

1. Give better item choice

You'll have to inquire as to whether this implies more assortment, greater product, or lower-estimated items. Perhaps the clients are inclined toward a specific brand they can't go anyplace else around. Prior to making an interest in extra stock, create sure there's gain potential in executing this idea. Adding new stock to your choice will possibly help your business assuming there are an adequate number of clients able to buy at costs that are productive to you.

2. Give longer active times

Clients need to have the option to shop when they have the

opportunity. That could mean being open later at night or prior toward the beginning of the day or at the end of the week. It could likewise mean booking arrangements for clients outside ordinary working hours. Perhaps they need to have the option to shop on the web. It could be an ideal opportunity to break down when clients really shop in your foundation then change your active times in like manner, or add web based shopping abilities to your site.

3. Great client support

Do you have at least some idea how your representatives treat clients when you're not there? Client assistance is the way into the verbal exchange promoting your desire to produce locally. You should seriously mull over employing a mysterious customer to give criticism on ways of further developing client support. Preparing can frequently assist workers with giving better client care. Your nearby Private company Advancement Center Organization most likely gives standard preparation open doors.

4. Acknowledge charge cards or checks, not simply cash

There are expenses engaged with charge cards or checks, so ensure you have laid out a productive evaluation that will take care of any expense increments. Train representatives in confirming that the check or Mastercard is great.

Clients purchase since they have needs, requirements, concerns or issues. Your business needs to fulfill the client while keeping up with productive tasks. Frequently entrepreneurs neglect to ask clients how to further develop their shopping experience next time they visit or regardless of whether there is anything more they need at the hour of procurement.

Clients frequently simply need to realize somebody is paying attention to them. Ask your clients for criticism and utilize that input to work on your business.

CHAPTER 5:

WHY THEY CHOOSE YOU

Any one of us could be to blame for not addressing favorable luck, particularly when it's surprising, and the equivalent goes for clients. You're reasonably only glad to have them there and, with that unusual gift horse expressing reverberating in your sub-conscience, don't remember to ask precisely the exact thing it was that carried them to you.

In any case, pinpointing what secured it for you more than one of your rivals isn't just an extraordinary proportion of how powerful your promoting, client care, and business the executives devices are, yet additionally a reasonable approach to giving yourself a merited congratulatory gesture.

The most effective way to figure out what carried your particular clients to you is to ask them! Overviews can give you loads of helpful information (top tip: offer an award draw for study members as a motivator) as can requesting that your clients leave you a survey. Yet, today we will check out at probably the most widely recognized things that influence a client in support of yourself.

1. They like your image

Late examination did via AirBnB has observed that the five vital qualities of a notorious brand are:
An in a split second unmistakable stylish - believe Starbucks' green goddess and natural stylistic theme
A widespread incentive

- Assuming a part in culture as opposed to simply reflecting it - think Apple driving society with innovation
- Representing something - a reason, an ideal
- Making a close to home association - like Disney, for instance

Clearly, only one out of every odd brand can be famous, however a solid brand will consolidate the greater part of these things somewhat. Your clients pick you since they like what your business relies on, how it introduces itself, both genuinely available and on the web, and how you do your own thing rather than indiscriminately pursuing directions.

2. Your administration was suggested

We as a whole realize that it generally will be valid that one good verbal exchange proposal from somebody you trust is worth in excess of a page of sparkling surveys on the web. So your client decided to come to you on the grounds that your client care was extraordinary and significant enough for their companion to educate them. Exceeding all expectations to give clients a striking encounter merits the time and exertion over the long haul, when your cup of excited evangelists runneth over and they fundamentally do your showcasing for you.

3. You have a dependability program

Maybe not as fulfilling a justification for your client returning to you, however compelling, is a certain financial motivator. Offering echo clients a prize for their dependability brings them once again to you by playing on the intrinsic love humanity has for a deal. Besides, a dedication stamp card resembles sending your own little delegate into the core of a client's regular routine, standing by without complaining in their satchel to say "Hi, recollect me? What about that free cut and blow dry?"

4. Web based booking

Alright, indeed, we would agree that this. In any case, tune in: web based booking truly is enormously alluring in addition to point for your business, and the end product speaks for itself. It's one of those undeniable characteristics of present day life that we as a whole have pretty comparative working hours, and that really intends that when we have the potential chance to book things, every other person is off the clock as well. Not so with web based booking, which allows your client to book any time or night, in any event, when your business is shut. That implies your business enjoys a programmed upper hand over each and every one of your rivals without web based booking.

5. You can characterize and use your upper hand

The initial step, as referenced, in advertising achievement, is distinguishing your strategic advantage. You really want to know how your business is giving answers for the commercial center. It may very well be the way your administration or item helps clients. It will likewise be the way your administration or item is not the same as the comparative administrations and items your immediate rival offers.

There will be different organizations that offer a similar item or administration as you do, particularly in the home administrations industry. Ponder why clients would be in an ideal situation picking your organization for that item or administration. Characterize your ideal interest group. Contemplate their requirements, needs, what they care about, and what challenges them? What might your item or administration do for them with those difficulties or address those issues and needs? How might your organization help your objective client? What advances of showing improvement over the rest?

Some of the time it isn't really that convoluted. Some of the time a client will pick your organization since it's helpful or they like your cost better. Indeed, even still, those things are the thing is giving you an upper hand in those circumstances. Characterizing your upper hand is the initial step.

6. You have a decent standing

Organizations that do legit, quality work will foster a decent standing. A strong standing in the commercial center will create more verbal exchange references, both on the web and off. On the off chance that you work really hard with one client, it is reasonable they will tell their companions, family, and even partners when inquired. Individuals will commonly pick an organization that has been suggested by somebody they trust, over an organization without that special interaction.

At a Canadian Home and Nursery Show before the end of last year, RenovationFind reviewed mortgage holders to decide how they are picking project workers for home remodels. 72.9% of members expressed that they track down redesign workers for hire by confiding in a reference from a companion. That is the vast majority. Building an uncommon standing by surpassing your client's assumptions will help you gain and hold new business.

Dealing with that standing reaches out to your web-based presence as well. While online client surveys are not generally dependable, they are still broadly utilized in shopper research. Nobody is awesome, thus regrettable surveys even happen to great organizations, yet the way in which you answered that audit is fundamental. At times organizations succumb to counterfeit audits, and you should be on top of that as well. Checking postings and audit destinations, and ensuring you answer concerns on the web, ought to be essential for your standing administration plan.

7. They can think that you are on the web

At the point when somebody is searching for another organization to enlist, the primary spot they will look for is on the web. In the event that your organization doesn't come up on Google query items, and they haven't caught wind of you from disconnected sources, they presumably won't track you down. Clearly, in the event that they can't find you, they can't pick you.

Putting time and cash in improving your web-based presence and site design improvement (Search engine optimization) is significant. Your Web optimization procedure could have many parts, including watchword investigation and examination, making content, utilizing online entertainment, building backlinks to your website, Pay-Per-Snap and other web publicizing, email showcasing, and a scope of other computerized   promoting exercises.

In the event that you don't have the opportunity or expertise to do any of these things yourself, employing an outsider Website optimization organization or a computerized   promoting organization to do it for you can be useful. Ensure your clients can think that you are on the web, or they may very well never track down you.

8. You give magnificent client care

Everybody needs to be dealt with well, particularly while putting resources into a critical remodel or costly item. Organizations who are well disposed, proficient, and speedy to answer clients will fabricate a standing for their administration. Assuming you are centered around your clients, they will feel dealt with and that you are assisting them with addressing their necessities or taking care of their concerns.

Awful client care will dissuade rehashing clients and references. It will probably bring about bad criticism and, surprisingly, terrible web-based surveys. Assuming you believe that your clients should deal with you with additional references and more business, you really want to treat them well.

9. You offer quality

Individuals care about quality, even in this present reality where modest comes fast and simple. The significance of putting resources into quality is particularly evident with regards to home redesigns. Mortgage holders would decide to spend somewhat more on a remodel work or item that is going to endure and address their issues as long as possible. Fleeting remodel administrations that accomplish ratty work don't keep going long around here. In the event that your organization centers around giving quality items and work, throughout saving time and above, you will end up being the unmistakable decision for the sort of client you need to draw in.

In a similar overview taken among mortgage holders at a Home and Nursery Show, the main things to property holders while picking a project worker were quality and reliability. These two contemplations were more essential to them than cost and client support.

10. You're dependable

Alongside quality, trust is fundamental. Being dependable is particularly fundamental in the home redesign industry. Everybody has heard an account of somebody being ripped off by a terrible project worker. Whether it was going home incomplete, making a junky showing, or totally taking off with their cash, it has been sufficient to make mortgage holders hesitant about employing workers for hire to work in their home. In the event that you can fabricate a standing of trust, and you do what you say you will do like clockwork, clients will pick you. Nobody will work with an organization that they can't confide in. Show that you're dependable, and you'll acquire new business.

11. The cost is correct

While the cost isn't overwhelmingly significant to customers, it is as yet a critical calculation navigation. A few customers will focus on a lower cost in their dynamic cycle. Notwithstanding, organizations that gain clients since they have the least cost will continuously lose clients when another person offers something for not exactly that. You won't increment the client unwaveringly with low costs, yet having cutthroat evaluating can be profitable.

Ensure your evaluation is fair. Remember that even absolute bottom evaluating can stop quality clients assuming they feel you're excessively modest. Similarly, in the event that you nickel and faint your clients at each opportunity you get, they will feel the sting. Offer them a serious, fair statement that separates all parts of your items and administrations. After you formalize a concurrence with the client, stick to it. Individuals will continuously be tense on the off chance that they believe they are being made the most monetarily yet won't avoid following through on a fair cost for remarkable help and items regardless of whether it is a greater cost than a contender.

12. It's the most helpful

Straightforward comfort is a justification for why customers could pick your business, regardless of whether they know nothing else about you. In some cases individuals are in a rush, and they can't be tried to do broad examinations on the organization they will recruit. Or on the other hand they need the task finished rapidly, and perhaps the most ideal organization for the gig has a bustling timetable, and they'll need to stand by. It may be the case that your organization truck was left at the perfect location with flawless timing, and they asked about a task without even a moment's pause. Or on the other hand perhaps this is on the grounds that your available time were more advantageous. In the event that you can offer something rapidly and bother free, clients could pick you no matter what different variables.

13. You have a common faith in a reason

In the event that you have confidence in what they trust in, a client could pick you over your rival. It doesn't need to be a strict conviction, however shared values and culture can fall into this classification. Assuming your organization provides for a specific cause, you could draw in potential clients who likewise support that foundation.

For that reason it is basic to remain associated with your neighborhood local area. In the event that you have a reason or association you're enthusiastic about it, appear for itself and spread the word. Supporting a reason locally could mean taking part in gathering pledges occasions or simply sharing their substance on your virtual entertainment takes care of. Assuming that what is essential to your client is critical to you, it can give you a benefit over contenders.

14. Clients can connect with your story.

For some purposes, the justification for what reason you're good to go and your story can influence them to pick your organization over their rivals. They could connect with the issue you've decided to tackle. Perhaps they can interface with your organization's story.

How about we utilize RenovationFind's story for instance. RenovationFind was made to help mortgage holders find and recruit confirmed, quality, and dependable exchanges and home remodel organizations. The business has gained notoriety for obscure workers for hire exploiting property holders. Thus, there was a need to make a framework that aided stop that issue.

That was one reason. As the second piece of that, great, commendable organizations were affected adversely by the discolored standing - and they should have been advanced as reliable, quality organizations to property holders so their business could develop. That is the second why RenovationFind started a new business.

For reasons unknown, property holders and remodel project workers could both connect with why RenovationFind started a new business. Property holders and workers for hire can both connect with why we do the things we do. Nobody needs to feel worried recruiting a home administrations organization since they figure they could get ripped off. No project worker needs to manage a terrible standing that they had no part in making. Their business shouldn't endure as a result of it, and they required a method for standing apart from the rest.

RenovationFind can give you an upper hand

RenovationFind is a free web based posting of pre-checked, confirmed exchanges, project workers, and home remodel organizations. Every one of the organizations on the registry meet severe measures and are observed ceaselessly to guarantee they're keeping up to norm. The measures incorporate legitimate and monetary record verifications, checking for permitting and protection, WCB inclusion, observing client surveys, and remunerating a higher positioning to the people who are a part on favorable terms with the Better Business Department.

At the point when your organization goes through this cycle, it shows clients that you are a project worker that offers quality and who can be relied upon. Having a wellspring of project workers in a single spot likewise makes it helpful for property holders to find you, not doing the historical verifications themselves. It scratches off a few of the ten reasons we have recorded why a client will pick you over a contender.

Notwithstanding an organization posting on the registry, a lot of computerized showcasing goes into assisting clients with tracking down you. Sites, web-based entertainment posts, pennant commercials, email advertising efforts, and site improvement are undeniably used to advance your industry and your particular organization. We take care of a very specialty market: home administrations, home redesigns, exchanges, and project workers.

RenovationFind has an enrollment base of a huge

number of property holders in your city, who all get computerized correspondence consistently. These individuals are offered limits from key joining forces organizations, and they know that employing workers for hire on RenovationFind is protected, helpful, and calm. We've accomplished the work to fabricate our standing and entrust with customers. At the point when an organization is on our index, they realize they can as of now trust it. In the event that you're RenovationFind Ensured, you naturally enjoy a serious upper hand over organizations in your industry who are not.

CHAPTER: 6

SELECT YOUR BRAND

It's difficult to fabricate a brand and support consistent development until you don't have a successful brand showcasing procedure set up. Organizations influence different promoting methodologies to extend their client base while keeping a respectable brand picture. One Google search can provide you with a heap of brand showcasing techniques from customary to present day. Some depend on your area, some work according to your financial plan, and the rundown goes on.

We are here to assist you with choosing brand showcasing methodologies for your business. However, before we plunge into that, we should characterize brand advertising since it's not equivalent to marking or showcasing.

What's an Image Promoting Procedure?

With regards to characterizing brand showcasing, it's a method for advancing your administrations or items by advancing your whole image. It's an essential method for advancing your image while recounting a story through your items or administrations.

Top worldwide brands use brand promoting to guarantee their clients stay related with the actual brand as opposed to a solitary item or administration. These strategies can be anything from a proactive slogan to selling a way of life alongside items. An ideal illustration of this would be Apple, which sells cell phones and a way of life with some great slogans, for example, Think Unique. Indeed, even Apple's white variety stylish matters a great deal since a mark tone can give a 80% lift to memorability.

Now that you realize brand advertising how about we go through a few helpful hints to choose your image promoting system.

Laying out a Brand Personality

Characterizing your image showcasing procedure initially requires you and your advertising group to respond to this multitude of inquiries significant for brand personality.

Questions you want to respond to include:

- What are the organization's fundamental beliefs and mission?
- Could you at any point portray your organization in only three words?

- How might you have an effect in your industry?
- How would you maintain that your image should look outwardly?
- For what you need to be known for in the commercial center?

Replies to these inquiries will assist you with deciding the uniqueness of your image and characterize objectives for your promoting techniques.

Deciding Brand Goals

The general purpose of formulating a brand methodology is to arrive at specific objectives and goals. You will have two choices before you, including short and long haul objectives. While the essential objective remaining parts brand advancement close to an expansion in deals, you can characterize where you need your image in a year or what numbers you anticipate after a specific time. For example, you might be searching for a place to be an industry chief through an expansion in client corporations, client standards for dependability, online item deals, and site visits.

Try to adjust your image advertising procedure with targets and business objectives.

Find out about Brand Crowd

Do you have any idea that more than 70% of brand advertisers keep deals and changes beneath, building a group of people? Your true capacity and current clients are your main interest group to fabricate serious areas of strength for a. Find out where they reside, their typical age, what items or administrations they have utilized, and their opinion on your business or brand. Get some information about things you can improve on for all time and keep them as your clients.

With definite information on your interest group, you can set your image showcasing procedure and appeal to your interest groups more.

Best Brand Advertising Practices

The way that 73% of individuals like a customized shopping experience from a brand can assist you with keeping a high client consistency standard. Building a brand demands investment since notoriety and believability fortifies a brand. From that point forward, you can circle back to modified messages, unique arrangements in light of your client's buy history, and more compelling promoting practices to construct a brand. We should move through a couple of common sense ways of cultivating faithfulness and entrust with your clients.

Center around Your Visual Game

While dealing with your image advertising methodology, having an ace-level visual game is basic. A HubSpot study recommends that the human mind processes visual data at a quicker rate than texts.

Visuals that mirror your business' basic beliefs and generally speaking brand topics are an imperative component of your image promoting methodology. It gives you consistency so your ongoing clients can distinguish you anyplace they see your items or administrations being promoted.

For example, we previously made sense of how Apple follows a white variety subject in the entirety of their items, bundling, and commercials to support their client commitment.

Selling a Story

Perhaps the best way that dress brands generally advance their items while helping their image mindfulness is by selling a story. The best model is Nike. The organization makes a move to transform an item sent off into a story. They even transform their thoughts into stories so clients can connect with them.

A narrating component in your promoting procedure really refines your image. You might believe there's nothing weighty in your story, yet all the same it's not necessary to focus on that. Just recounting your business story, where you came from, and how a specific item transformed into the truth is sufficient to impact and change over likely clients.

Steady Item and Brand Personality

On-brand upgrades ought to be a long-lasting piece of your

showcasing procedure, yet you don't need to change your image character and item consistency. The best illustration of this procedure is a 60+-year-old brand that actually "satisfies you." McDonald's has rolled out exceptionally minor improvements to its logo, items, or whatever else since its beginning. Indeed, even their different promoting slogans at last passed on a similar message-satisfaction with their food.

As a sharp business person or advertiser, you are likely pondering: how might I separate my image from an unendingly considerable rundown of vicious contenders?

The short response is marking Regardless of whether you're effectively dealing with your image character, it exists. Furthermore, the possibilities emerging as the ideal decision to your potential clients lays on major areas of strength for how solid your image is. Making a logo and that snappy trademark isn't sufficient, yet at the same simply the start. To stick out, you really want to go past these and incorporate fundamental components that characterize your business quite a long while ahead.

Here, we'll cover:

Why marking your business is significant.

The most effective method to mark your business in seven stages.

Instances serious areas of strength for and what we can gain from them.

For what reason is it critical to mark your business?

Despite size, associations of different types need to put resources into marking to remain pertinent. Assuming that you're actually asking why you ought to mark your business, here are a few advantages you stand to acquire.

1. Recognize your business from rivals.

With the heap of organizations conveying comparable administrations or items, standing apart can challenge. That is where marking comes in. Your qualities, story, brand guarantee, and different resources give roads through which you can exhibit your uniqueness. Utilizing these to make a place of distinction could separate you from your rivals.

2. Turn out to be more conspicuous.

One more advantage of putting resources into a predictable marking exertion is to make your image more vital. At the point when clients can distinguish your organization in view of physical, visual, hear-able components, it breeds commonality. This encourages trust, which 81% of clients depend on to pursue a purchasing choice. Memorability could likewise impact how clients review and draw in with your substance, messages, or advertisements.

3. Construct client reliability.

Strong brands frequently have a faithful client base, however it doesn't occur by some coincidence. It originates from conveying one of a kind encounters and informing their crowds can relate with to frame a bond. With this profound association, you'll have more clients who will uphold your business and offer their positive encounters. This benefit could mean recurrent business, not so much agitation, but rather more references through informal.

4.   Acquire   and   hold representatives.

As indicated by LinkedIn, organizations with a solid boss brand will draw in half more qualified competitors 1-2 times quicker than others. Additionally, they'll select at half less expense per enlist. Dropping down to your current and past representatives, their experience, and what they spread the news means for your work environment notoriety and representative degrees of consistency.

Whether you're hoping to recruit gifted engineers and other particular jobs or looking to get your best ability far from contenders, effectively dealing with your image isn't a choice. It is a need.

Follow these means for marking your business

As may be obvious, building your image doesn't need to be overpowering or costly. A large portion of these tips cost hardly anything. You can begin with a thin financial plan and afterward scale your marking endeavors as your organization develops. Follow these seven straightforward moves toward brand your business:

- Distinguish your ideal interest group
- Make your offer
- Decide your main goal
- Characterize your image character
- Make brand resources
- Coordinate them across your channels
- Be predictable.

The most effective method to mark your business in 7 stages

So how would you approach fostering a reliable character and style behind your business? We should separate it into seven stages.

1. Distinguish your crowd

The initial step for marking your business is to comprehend who your potential clients are. There are a couple of moves toward this interaction.

Investigate your ongoing client base

Existing clients are a goldmine of data as they probably are aware that it is noteworthy or ailing in your image. Find their inclinations and requirements.

What is their most squeezing trouble spot?

Which organizations do they trust and purchase from?

What might they very much want to find in your image?

You can connect with clients straightforwardly through calls and overviews or study them to track down replies. Chances are, you'll find normal qualities or examples that will assist you with characterizing your interest group.

Direct statistical surveying

Statistical surveying can assist you with revealing industry patterns, potential open doors, client inclinations, purchasing propensities, and discussions about your image or others. Likewise, it's a successful method for social event data on your opposition. Note who their clients are, favored channels, interests, and so forth. Pertinent virtual entertainment channels, audit locales, industry discussions, or question and answer session destinations like Reddit are incredible spots to begin your exploration.

Make purchaser personas

Bunch clients in view of examples or normal characteristics you reveal and address them with a persona. Incorporate segment, psychographic, social, and geographic subtleties.

2. Make your offer

Your offer is your image guarantee. It is more than a slogan or a motto. An UVP depicts how your answer can take care of the issues of your ideal clients better than contenders. To create a strong incentive, contemplate the accompanying:

How might your item or administration address their problem(s)?

What elements spur their purchasing choices?

For what reason do your current clients pick your business over your rivals?

Make a special offering suggestion with replies to these inquiries utilizing the voice of your clients. Convey benefits, what you plan to convey, and why they ought to pick you over contenders. Adhere to reality with no superfluous publicity.

3. Decide your main goal and fundamental beliefs

For what reason does your business exist? Your central goal addresses this inquiry. To compose a strong statement of purpose, portray the reason for your business, who your clients are, the items or administrations you render, and how you make it happen. Sum up this in a couple of words to make it essential. Here is an illustration of a statement of purpose.

Next up are your basic beliefs. They are rules that drive your objectives, mission, and vision. These convictions shape your organization culture, which then impacts partners' insights. In this way, utilizing conventional words that don't characterize what your business relies on will just prompt a clashing brand picture. All things considered, be explicit, utilize your own words, and guarantee the whole association epitomizes these standards.

4. Characterize your image character

Your image character, very much like that of a person's, is a blend of characteristics that your association displays. In a perfect world, these qualities will draw in individuals to your organization and shape their discernments. In this manner, a character that reverberates with your clients could assist you with building a profound association and stand apart from contenders.

Consider the characteristics you'd very much want to connect with your image. Would you like to be viewed as visionary, equipped, or charming? Pick your qualities and the voice you'll speak with. For instance, assuming that your image character is rough, your image voice could be certain and solid.

This rundown of profound words and expressions might help you in this cycle.

5. Make brand resources

The following stage is to pick the components that will distinguish your business. A few models are colors, text styles, bundling, trademark, and your logo. Certain varieties inspire explicit feelings and convey implications. For instance, The Logo Organization recommends that red lifts energy levels, yellow is idealism, and purple enacts the creative mind.

Whichever logo, variety plan, and style you decide to mark your business, guarantee that it is particular and effectively conspicuous. Converse with specialists and your group and play around with logo creators (like Looka, for instance) to get a few thoughts.

6. Incorporate them across your channels

Presently your marking components are prepared, and circulate them across your channels. For instance, you can incorporate visual resources like your logo, varieties, and text styles in the entirety of your informing. A lengthier form of your statement of purpose could act as your image story on the About Us page.

Despite the fact that your basic beliefs will for the most part stay inside your site, you could likewise edify clients and expected workers on a big motivator for you through marked recordings and posts. Remember that marking is a continuous cycle however long your organization exists.

7. Be predictable

As indicated by MarketingNutz, it takes up to 5-7 brand impressions before an individual can review your image. From the site to online entertainment channels and disconnected connections with clients, marking should be steady. Make brand rules to support cohesiveness.

Is your image voice energetic and relaxed on socials? Then there's a compelling reason you should be firm on your websites. Your clients ought to know what's in store or feel once they see your substance, logos, or other brand resources. Consistency fabricates commonality, trust, and faithfulness. These sentiments reflect fruitful marking.

Instances of organizations with a solid brand personality

We should see a few existing organizations with a solid brand character and tips you can use for your organization.

1. Float

A well known conversational promoting stage, Float tries to rethink how B2B deals discussions happen. With its initiative rule of "Put the client at the focal point of all that you do," the organization centers around quick human-to-human connection.

Through Float, organizations can have customized discussions with clients continuously as opposed to through the customary rubbing inclined strategy for lead structures and vast messages.

The organization satisfies its client driven values by drawing in with its clients similarly. Float's center qualities are human, energetic, and striking. This is noticeable in its engaging online courses, web journals, and showcasing materials conveyed across channels with proficient yet language free words.

Key action item:

Your qualities and UVP are not simply words. They are commitments and activities which the whole association ought to satisfy.

2. Zopa

Fintech organizations are normally a smidgen excessively intense, yet Zopa remains out of sight. Zopa offers fixed-term reserve funds and shared loaning administrations to clients across the UK.

The brand conveys instructive and engaging monetary substance to supporters in an idiosyncratic, funny however proficient way. It makes their substance effectively edible even to a non-monetarily educated crowd. Likewise, the organization keeps a predictable tone and variety plot from their social records to their site.

Key focus point:

Don't hesitate for even a moment to investigate a character that may not be famous inside your specialty. However long it's sensible and is one your clients might connect with, try it out. In the meantime, be certain not to mistake your crowd for momentary changes. Remain steady.

3. ASOS

The web based business brand ASOS portrays itself as true, bold, innovative, and restrained. This multitude of characteristics are noticeable in its product and content. ASOS plans to. This makes sense of why its substance is cheeky, energetic, and locking in. From the statement of purpose to the Twitter bio and ordinary posts, the informing matches a brand that serves recent college grads and more seasoned Gen Zs. The reaction they get plainly shows that the substance reverberates with its crowd.

Key action item: The force of engaging substance is colossal. Figure out your interest group and make drawings that can assist summon sentiments and construct a relationship with clients.

CHAPTER 7:

CAPTURING LEADS

Most deals experts expect to find drivers, who are people with the possibility to become clients. One famous method for finding and coordinating potential customers is to utilize a lead catch, which is a structure that accumulates data about people who may be successful leads. Getting familiar with what lead catches are and the way that you can use them to further develop lead age might assist you with meeting your deals objectives.

In this article, we survey what lead catch is, the way to make a lead catch arrangement and how you can make progress with lead catch.

What Is Lead Capturing?

Lead capturing is a method for social event data about people who show interest in an organization and could become clients later on. There are a couple strategies for making a lead catch, yet one of the most well-known ways of utilizing them is to make a structure that offers clients the chance to present their own data to an organization, like their name, address and contact data. Lead catches can show up on organization sites, virtual entertainment stages, messages and blog entries.

Why use lead catch on your site? Lead catch can be significant for any business that sells items or administrations since it gives an incredible method for laying out and growing a client base. With lead catch, you can take data from expected clients and use it to reach them in the future to offer insights concerning items you deal with and welcome them to make buys with your organization.

Lead catch is likewise significant on the grounds that catches can go about as extra advertising instruments. You can utilize lead catch as a source of inspiration (CTA) that welcomes customers to connect with your organization's site and perhaps make a purchase.

For instance, you could make a lead catch with the target of procuring a specific number of deals for a particular item or drawing in more rush hour gridlock to an organization site. Both of these targets are explicit and feasible, however they can likewise add to the general objective of producing prospective customers.

Step by step instructions to Make A B2B LEAD Catching Methodology

Not certain where to begin with your B2B lead catching methodology? Here are a moves toward assist you with beginning:

1. Characterize your lead catching goal

Priorities straight — what's the target of your lead catch?

To create all the more delicate leads? Get more bulletin information exchanges? Download an aide? Secure more deals and gatherings?

While the overall objective is to eventually create more income, the kind of satisfied composed and conveyed is fundamental for figuring out where the possibility or lead is in their B2B deals excursion, and how you believe they should manage the data given to them. Regardless, your target is essential to characterize it so you can gauge its adequacy over the long haul.

2. Sort out what you maintain that your deal should be

What do you maintain that clients should acquire from presenting their data to your business? Subsequent to deciding the objective YOU need from your B2B lead catching methodology, what do you believe the LEAD should acquire?

Lead catching ought to be a commonly helpful connection among you and a likely purchaser. The main justification behind them to present their own data is to acquire something consequently.

For instance, to get more pamphlet recruits so you can sustain the relationship with the lead over the long haul, they're hoping to get month to month or every other month bulletins to study your item or administration contributions or acquire knowledge into your industry mastery.

Anything that you pick your proposal to be, you should ensure it lines up with your general substance methodology and what you need to accomplish from these lead catch endeavors. For instance, assuming that you request that clients give you their contact data for pamphlets, yet you don't really have organization bulletins, this gives no advantage or worth to your business, or the leaders.

3. Make a lead catch greeting page and promotion

Now that you've laid out an objective and what you believe leads should acquire from your endeavors, now is the ideal time to make your lead catch greeting page, promotion duplicate, and structure fill prerequisites.

The greeting page ought to be drawing in and line up with what your definitive objective is for the client. On the off chance that it doesn't line up with their purpose of the lead catch, they'll without a doubt dismiss. This expands the gamble of bob rates which adversely influence your mission and return on initial capital investment.

The equivalent goes for your promotion duplicate. Promotion duplicate for your lead catch ought to acquaint clients with what they're expecting when they click on the advertisement. On the off chance that your promotion and presentation page aren't adjusted, you're not furnishing the client with the client experience they were expecting, bringing about low change rates.

Also, ultimately, contingent upon the promotion and presentation page made, it's critical to consider what the contact structure ought to resemble. On the off chance that it's an all the more delicate lead for an aide download or bulletin join, the contact structure necessities ought to most likely be more limited and incorporate the complete name and company email of the client so you gain the data you want without overpowering the client.

Then again, assuming the lead catch is more deals driven and transformation engaged, the contact structure ought to be longer so you have all the data you want to guarantee they're prepared to purchase. The more data they're willing to give you, the more probable they most likely are to make a buy.

4. Dole out a stage for your lead catch approach

In this step, now is the right time to dole out a stage to your lead catch endeavors. Your B2B lead catch technique ought to look and be changed relying upon the stage you're appointing them to.

On the off chance that it's a Google Promotion lead catch, it ought to be more transformation engaged, empowering prompts to plan a business meeting or make a buy. Then again, in the event that it's a social promotion lead catch, it's without a doubt empowering prompts download a free, selective aide or pursue bulletins.

Notwithstanding, it's critical to dole out a lead catch stage in view of the personas of your objective market. For instance, in the event that most purchasers in your objective market are bound to change over on your site, it's fundamental to require your investment zeroing in on site lead catch versus social.

5. Screen and change your lead catch System Depending on the situation

Furthermore, similar to some other B2B lead age approaches, you should screen your B2B lead catch endeavors and cause acclimations to your methodology as they appear to be fit. This enables your advertising and lead age groups to give deals higher changing over leads.

Best lead capturing strategies for b2b lead age groups to follow

The means recorded above aren't sufficient to construct a lead catching methodology that yields results. To take advantage of your lead catch endeavors, ensure your B2B lead age groups follow these prescribed procedures:

Utilize different kinds of lead magnets

Few out of every odd chief who runs over your organization is in a similar phase of the B2B lead age and promoting pipe, which makes executing different sorts of lead magnets fundamental for getting the ideal leads with flawless timing.

For instance, assuming you notice that your aide downloading lead magnets aren't producing an adequate number of leads, consider changing it into a pamphlet or an alternate kind of lead magnet. Or then again on the off chance that your social lead catch endeavors aren't acquiring any effect, it merits trying out different stages to advance your business and the bits of knowledge you bring to the table.

A/B test different contact structure fills

As referenced before, contingent upon the B2B lead catch objective, it's critical to adjust the contact structure with what they're searching for and consider their stage in the purchasing cycle. Assuming that there are excesses of structure fill necessities, you risk dismissing clients on the off chance that they're not prepared to change over. Then again, in the event that you have excessively barely any, you risk creating bad quality leads who aren't prepared to change over.

Incorporate multi step lead catch structuresIf your change centered lead catch methodology requires a ton of data however is having an issue creating leads, consider utilizing multi step lead catch structures. As opposed to having all the structure top necessities on a solitary pop-off and possibly overpowering the client, multistep lead catch structures make the structure fill prerequisites less scary, expanding the quantity of leads created from your lead catch endeavors.

Carry out chatbots to connect more web guests

Quite possibly the quickest developing way that B2B organizations are catching leads is by executing chatbots on their site to connect more clients and assist with driving them to what they're searching for. Chatbots were once considered a client support device (which they actually are), yet they can be considerably more than that. By utilizing chatbots for lead catch, you can:

Further develop site client experience

Successfully catch leads nonstop

Upgrade lead capability endeavors

Support client commitment

Chatbots can likewise be utilized as a live visit stage, permitting deals improvement reps to talk one-on-one with clients to realize what they're searching for and how your organization can help. This can assist them with better qualifying drives before they're shipped off your outreach group.

WAYS OF IMPROVING YOUR B2B LEAD Catching Technique

Assuming you've been rehearsing lead catching for a little while however aren't getting the effect you need, there are a few different ways that you can streamline your system. The following are a couple of the top ways you can enhance your **B2B lead catching methodology:**

consider the progression of the client excursion. Perhaps the greatest ruin that promoting and lead-age experience isn't thinking about the progression of the client excursion and how they explore all through the B2B deals pipe. In the event that your lead catching endeavors are occurring beyond where the client is in their purchaser process, you won't get a similar effect.

For instance, assuming that a leader is on a site administration page and prepared to change over, giving them a spring up that urges them to download an aide won't encourage them to contact your business and timetable a deals meeting. Then again, in the event that you have an over the top selling-zeroed in lead catch on an enlightening piece of content on your site or social profile, you risk dismissing the client from your business since they feel excessively wrecked.

Portion and target lead catching endeavors

Instead of essentially sharing and advancing lead magnets across your objective market, consider sectioning and focusing on them in view of the different purchaser personas inside your crowd. On the off chance that you give a designated and customized insight to chiefs, they're bound to change over in light of the fact that they see themselves in these promotions.

For instance, we should recommend that you're a business cleaning organization that needs to create more clients in the schooling area. For this situation, you could advance LinkedIn lead catching promotions designated at school directors and office administrators about your schooling centered cleaning administrations. This urges them to contemplate their ongoing arrangement and investigate how your business could be a superior fit for their tasks since you explicitly recommended master school cleaning administrations.

A/B test your presentation page, promotion duplicate, and structure fills

A/B testing (or split testing) your lead catching methodology is fundamental for seeing what works and what doesn't. This can incorporate split testing lead catch configuration, promotion duplicate, call-to-activities (CTAs), symbolism, and that's only the tip of the iceberg.

As we examined before, there are many accepted procedures your advertising and lead age groups can follow to help the quantity of leads produced. Evaluating these various techniques can assist you with boosting your lead catch procedure. For instance, give testing a shot:

A multistep versus long-structure contact structure fill

The quantity of structure fill necessities

Chatbot informing (and where it drives clients)

Delicate lead-or change centered lead catching endeavors

Key Important Points

To connect more leads in your objective market, you should have a B2B lead catching methodology set up. Without it, you risk passing up critical open doors from leaders who are effectively searching for an answer for their trouble spots

Tips for fruitful lead catch

The following are a couple of ways to direct a lead catch:

Utilize various types of lead catches:- There are one or two kinds of lead catches that a business can use to produce potential customers. While the most well-known may be to make a lead catch page on an organization site, you can likewise configure lead catches that gather client data over email, from calls or from direct messages via virtual entertainment stages. Involving at least one elective strategy for lead catches can upgrade your advertising drive by growing the gathering of purchasers you can reach.

Consider the fields you use in your structure:- While making a lead catch page, pondering the fields you need to remember for the structure that clients use to present their own data can assist with ensuring your lead catch is succinct and just proposes significant subtleties. This can smooth out the most common way of finishing up a lead catch structure for clients and can help make investigating lead catch shapes a simple and fast interaction. For instance, assuming your lead catch targets buyers in the overall population, you could focus on fields that pay attention to contact data and way of life propensities as opposed to subtleties like work title or industry.

Screen your wellsprings of traffic:- In light of the fact that a lead catch regularly works on a specific stage, it tends to be critical to consider how much traffic that source could practically draw in. There are numerous ways of monitoring how much traffic a site or page encounters, for example, checking on a page's presentation in web search tool results and recording the quantity of collaborations posts on an organization's site get. When you comprehend where the greater part of your traffic comes from, you can plan your lead catch to show up on that particular stage to reach whatever number of potential prospective customers as could be expected under the circumstances.

CHAPTER 8:

NURTURING LEADS

What is nurturing leads?

Lead nurturing is when organizations fabricate associations with possibilities. It is a significant part of inbound advertising, which is the utilization of content showcasing, virtual entertainment and other web-based specialized techniques to stand out for clients. At the point when a potential client finds your business, they may not be prepared to buy your items or administrations. Supporting leads is a compelling procedure for driving deals, since it can keep you top of mind for possibilities so they return when they are prepared to buy.

Lead sustaining is like any relationship: The more you put into it, the more you receive in return. However, on the off chance that you neglect to fortify a relationship, you'll normally float separated, lead supporting is the most common way of building associations with possibilities.

What is the significance of supporting your leads?

Albeit a definitive objective of lead sustaining is to drive deals, it offers a few different advantages:

Acquaints possibilities with your organization

Lead support is a successful method for showing possibilities for your administrations and items. You might not have sufficient room on a greeting page to really make sense of the effect of your items and administrations, yet lead sustaining permits you to show potential clients a more complete image of what your identity is and how you can help them.

Assists you with acquiring your crowd's trust. Showing your potential clients that you comprehend their problem areas or giving them valuable tips can assist you with interfacing with your crowd and gain their trust. Sharing your insight tells them that your relationship isn't just about your organization making a deal yet in addition about furnishing them with essential devices and data.

Makes you an ideal chief.

As you make smart, significant substance and correspondences, lead sustaining can support your standing and assist you with being viewed as a forerunner in your industry.

Assist your crowd with recollecting that you. In the event that you discuss your possibilities, they will probably recollect you. Remaining top of the brain is particularly useful so they will go to you when they need or need your items or administrations.

Reinforces your deals technique. Outreach groups are generally centered around selling at the time, and that implies numerous potential clients aren't being focused on. Lead sustaining offers you the chance to target future clients.

Diminishes client obtaining costs.

Lead age permits you to go to more affordable strategies for drawing in clients, and saving on showcasing is really great for your client procurement costs (CAC = complete advertising cost/number of deals).

Increments deals.

With lead sustaining, you can transform possibilities into better leads. As a matter of fact, sustained leads make buys that are 47% greater than non-supported drives, Annuitas detailed in view of exploration from Promoting Sherpa.

Were you aware?

Lead support is significant for expanding deals, yet it can likewise assist you with working on your organization's standing and gain your crowd's trust.

Seven compelling lead-sustaining procedures

There are a lot of systems you can use to sustain leads, yet remember that they can change after some time. A technique you effectively used to draw in with your possibilities in the past may not work from here on out.

The following are seven powerful techniques for supporting leads:

1. Use email promoting.

55% of advertisers say email promoting drives the best yield on venture of all computerized showcasing systems, as per research from Mission Screen.

In addition to the fact that email promoting is more practical than publicizing, yet it can likewise be customized through information and client conduct research. Email division, or the division of email endorsers into more modest gatherings in view of various boundaries, permits you to actually target leads more.

For instance, assuming your organization made a digital book, you could send it just to supporters who have drawn in with past digital books or comparable substance, since they are bound to invite it. If you somehow managed to send it to your whole email show, a few beneficiaries wouldn't open it and could try and be irritated by getting an additional email, which would harm your relationship.

2. Email division is flexible.

You can target clients as per the items they peruse, the sort of happiness they download, where they are in the deals channel, what messages they open and that's just the beginning. As you get more data about your possibilities, you'll have the option to make more-customized messages.

As well as fragmenting messages to increment commitment, you ought to do the accompanying:

Keep the title short, and ensure it sticks out.

Invest energy composing a convincing review text.

- Add suggestions to take action (CTAs).
- Be succinct.
- Make your messages dynamic.
- Send significant messages.
- Urge possibilities to answer.
- A/B test however much as could reasonably be expected.

One more advantage of email supporting is that you can computerize it. With the right apparatuses, you can undoubtedly make email records, as well as timetable messages when it's generally advantageous for you.

Remember that with this system, you should figure out some kind of harmony. You need to speak with your crowd routinely so that you're constructing a relationship yet not time after time that they feel you are spamming them.

3. Work out your substance promoting.

Content promoting is an inconceivably valuable methodology that rotates around making content, for example, blog entries, digital books, FAQs, how-to articles, online courses, research reports and the sky's the limit from there. You can utilize this substance to fabricate brand mindfulness and attract more individuals.

Content promoting additionally takes care of into your other lead-supporting systems. For instance, you can utilize online entertainment and email to disseminate the substance you produce. Or on the other hand, you can add CTAs, for example, empowering perusers to pursue your pamphlet or connecting for more data.

Content advertising can likewise assist with working on your organization's standing. Through happiness, you can show that you are concerned and grasp your possibilities' requirements. Rather than focusing exclusively on your own items and administrations, you can move the concentration onto your expected clients.

Utilizing the deals channel, you can represent various leads' necessities. There are three phases in the deals channel:

4. Mindfulness (top of the channel).

This stage starts after an individual comes into contact with your organization and associates here and there. As of now, they may simply be finding out about your business and its items and administrations. You ought to try to grasp likely clients' requirements. This stage fits blog entries, web-based entertainment posts, digital broadcasts, digital books, recordings and infographics.

Thought (center of the channel). In this stage, things begin to get more serious. Potential clients might start to comprehend how your items or administrations could function for them, and they begin to think about buying them. This is a great opportunity to fabricate entrust with your leads. You can draw in them with occasions, online classes, messages, whitepapers and contextual analyses.

5. Buy (lower part of the pipe).

This is the point at which you convince your prompts to buy from you, and it's an amazing chance to make faithful clients. Content in this stage incorporates coupons, item includes, use cases, item examination pages, tributes and valuing pages.

While it means quite a bit to ponder focusing on your crowd while you're making content, you'll likewise need to ensure you are making great substance. Find these ways to upgrade your substance procedure endeavors:

Think of a substance plan.

Center around quality.

Use catchphrases to track down pertinent themes.

Stay away from catchphrase stuffing.

Compose for people, not calculations.

Check for syntactic blunders.

Make applicable substances.

Guarantee your substance has esteem.

Compose web crawler enhanced content.

Share your substance on your different channels.

Get dynamic via online entertainment.

Online entertainment is a viable method for building associations with possibilities. It gives them a simple method for conversing with you, and it likewise puts your substance where many individuals invest their energy.

You can utilize virtual entertainment to convey your substance and to show a portion of your image's character.

Follow these tips to succeed at virtual entertainment:

- Update your substance consistently.
- Present the right happy on the right virtual entertainment channel.
- Talk with your crowd.
- Study for your examination.
- Figure out your crowd.
- Be aware of patterns.

- Use instruments to robotize and work on the interaction.
- Consider beginning a record devoted to client care.

You can likewise utilize web-based entertainment to retarget advertisements. After potential clients leave your site, they might disregard your items and administrations, yet friendly retargeting can remind them about your business.

Adjust deals, promoting and client service groups.

Supporting leads is a collaboration. Deals and client service groups find out about an organization's crowd firsthand, and the showcasing group has a ton of noteworthy information.

Compelling coordinated effort among these groups will bring about better knowledge, which will prompt improved arrangements.

6. Direct reviews.

To fabricate an association with your leads, you should figure out their necessities. Reviews permit prompts let you know what they feel in a way that would sound natural to them. In the event that you get some information about their objectives or the issues they face, you'll have the option to make an arrangement for how to get them to the furthest limit of the purchaser's excursion.

7. Score leads.

Lead scoring allows you to relegate a worth, frequently mathematical, to your leads in light of their ways of behaving.

Since few out of every odd lead will be in similar phase of the deals pipe, you shouldn't focus on each possibility. For instance, your lead-scoring model might dole out additional focuses to possibilities who invest energy perusing your site and have higher navigate rates, and less focus to the individuals who have pursued a pamphlet yet seldom open messages. Your endeavors will probably have a greater effect on the off chance that you center around the possibilities who are drawing in with you.

You can attempt to interface with the individuals who score exceptionally on a more private level, for example, by having an agent contact them.

Circle back to your leads after you make the deal.

Lead support doesn't end after the deal. After a client has purchased your item or administration, you believe they should make want more, since they are probably going to burn through three fold the amount of as one-time clients.

CHAPTER: 9

FOCUS ON IT

A center system is a strategy for creating, showcasing and offering items to a specialty market, which could be a sort of shopper, product offering or geological region. A spotlight system would fixate on the extension of showcasing strategies for your organization while planning to lay out another relationship with your interest group. If a promoting organization had any desire to procure outsider validity, they would need to have advertising integrated with their center technique to get articles distributed and fabricate their image.

A center technique adjusts an organization's items and promotes to its designated crowd. Coming up with an effective center technique will assist an association with figuring out its client's needs and needs so they can create items they will buy and see as helpful.

In this article, we will distinguish what a center technique is, and depict the means important to create a center system that will make a brand stand apart from its specialty crowd.

Step by step instructions to build a center methodology

On the off chance that an organization is attempting to scale their business, think about these moves toward working out a center methodology:

- Gather a SWOT investigation.
- Produce a five power examination to grasp market contests.

- Contrast SWOT investigation and the five powers examination.
- Decide the objectives and target market of the methodology.

Check arrangement of key and authoritative objectives.

1. Incorporate a swot investigation

A SWOT investigation finds an association's assets, shortcomings, open doors and dangers. It assists with knowing who to target at first, however directing a SWOT investigation features the subtleties of each forthcoming business sector.

The following are a couple of test inquiries to pose while dealing with a SWOT examination.

Qualities:

Which clients have bought our item previously?

Is that interest group actually purchasing from us?

Assuming this is the case, what triumphs might we at any point apply to other objective business sectors?

How might developing a relationship with this specialty crowd construct our image?

Shortcomings:

Does the interest group have some familiarity with the item?

Assuming this is the case, will they think the item is functional for them to utilize?

Does this ideal interest group have a positive involvement in the item?

Is more capital or innovation expected to tempt this crowd?

Valuable open doors:

- Do current market patterns demonstrate great in drawing in this crowd?
- Are there occasions inside the region that the organization can benefit from?
- Provided that this is true, what will be their response when you approach them about the item?
- Might powerhouses at any point draw in clients to the item?

Dangers:

- Which contenders can impact this crowd and how?

- Will innovative progressions influence the advertising methodology pushing ahead?
- Will purchaser's reactions to showcase patterns influence the association?
- What expected advancements in the market can hurt the connection between the organization and the objective market?

2. Produce a five powers examination to grasp market rivalry

In 1979, Michael Watchman, a teacher from Harvard College, made Doorman's Five Powers as a device to survey and look at an industry's opposition and productivity. Today, it is one of the most well known devices for business procedure. In the event that you produce a rundown of the five powers, it will give an association the devices it wants to concentrate on the opposition, limit their specialty markets of revenue and believe about how coordinated operations should be done once another market is picked.

Doorman's five powers include:

Serious Competition:

- What number of opponents does an organization have?
- Who are rivals in the business?
- Is their item quality practically identical to the remainder of the business?

Provider Power:

- What number of potential providers are there?
- How one of a kind is the item or administration given?
- Is it costly to switch providers?
- **Purchaser Power:**
- What number of purchasers are there?
- Do purchasers buy huge orders?
- What is the expense of exchanging items over to the association's adversary?

Danger of Replacement:

- Could clients at any point find an alternate method for doing what an organization does?

- Might this help at any point be rethought or done physically?
- How modest could this replacement be for the contender?

Danger of New Section:
- How effectively can individuals enter the business?
- Can they lay out a traction once they enter?
- Will guidelines smother development of new rivalry?

3. Contrast SWOT examination and the five powers investigation

When all information is accumulated from the exploration, analyze the data from the SWOT examination and the five powers investigation and pick which key choices are helpful for progress. Likewise, go through essential choices or speculative situations with a gathering to find the outcomes in the event that you extended promoting assets to a specific specialty crowd. An association can ask themselves how their procedure:

Fabricates and supports a relationship with interest groups

Isolates an organization from its opposition

Use purchaser, provider and client power

Obstructs dangers of replacement or new passage to the market

4. Decide the objectives of the center methodology

Objective setting will assist with setting clear targets for where an organization goes. Without them, there is no immediate course in deciding the capability of an item or brand. With the Brilliant (Explicit, Quantifiable, Feasible, Pertinent and Time sensitive) system, you can decide the time and assets expected to arrive at organization objectives and impact the perfect individuals.

The following is an illustration of how you can execute this equation.

The organization will have a 90 percent consumer loyalty rate in one year once the item is carried out in January.

Explicit: The objective of expanding consumer loyalty is plainly stamped.

Quantifiable: Achievement can be estimated by the quantity of overviews with positive input, web-based entertainment bits of knowledge observing client conduct, and so on.

Reachable: The organization knows an opportunity to carry out the item.

Pertinent: The organization is anticipating hitting its imprint after the item goes available.

Time sensitive:

The organization has a one-year time span to meet its objective.

5. Confirm arrangement of key and hierarchical objectives

Subsequent to choosing objectives from the center methodology, carve out opportunity to assess assuming the essential objectives meet long haul hierarchical targets. Long haul hierarchical objectives consolidate the association's cutthroat position recorded in the five powers examination, productivity, profit from speculation and the organization's picture in the public eye.

On the off chance that an organization needs assistance

with tracking down their ideal interest group, start by starting statistical surveying techniques, for example, center gatherings and online reviews.

In general, a center methodology is an advantage for an organization hoping to grow its arrive at inside various business sectors. Following this strategy will assist an association with adjusting to the different changes of an industry's cutthroat scene, other than the ideal interest group's guiding principle, perspectives and ways of behaving.

Why You Ought to Concentrate Your Showcasing Methodology

In the business world, there's generally the compulsion to attempt to be everything to everybody. All things considered, on the off chance that you can offer your item or administration to additional individuals, then, at that point, you'll get more cash-flow, correct?

Truly attempting to be everything to everybody is a catastrophe waiting to happen. You'll wind up burning through a large chunk of change on showcasing without obtaining the outcomes you need.

All things considered, you really want to concentrate on showcasing your methodology. By zeroing in on a particular objective market, you can make a more compelling promoting effort that will contact the ideal individuals and create more deals.

The following are four motivations behind why you ought to concentrate your promoting methodology:

1. You'll Set aside Cash

At the point when you attempt to speak to everybody, you wind up squandering a large chunk of change. You could purchase promoting space in a wide range of news sources or make a showcasing effort that is expansive to the point that it doesn't actually say anything.

Conversely, when you center your promoting methodology, you can spend your cash all the more carefully. You'll know precisely where to promote and how to arrive at your objective market. Therefore, you'll get all the more value for your money.

2. You'll Contact The Ideal Public

Then again, when you center your showcasing system, you can make a message that reverberates with your objective market. Thus, you're bound to contact individuals who are really keen on what you bring to the table.

3. You'll Stand Apart From The Opposition

In the present swarmed commercial center, it's a higher priority than any time in recent memory to stand apart from the opposition. Assuming you attempt to be everything to everybody, you'll mix in with different organizations that are all attempting to do exactly the same thing.

Be that as it may, assuming that you center your advertising methodology, you can make your business stick out. You can situate yourself as the go-to supplier for your objective market and separate yourself from your rivals.

4. You'll Realize Your Clients Better

At the point when you attempt to be everything to everybody, it's hard to get to truly know your clients. All things considered, on the off chance that you're attempting to interest everybody, you're not exactly centered around any one gathering.

Then again, when you center your promoting system, you can find out about your objective market. You can figure out what they need and need and make a showcasing effort that addresses their issues. Therefore, you'll fabricate more grounded associations with your clients.

Center around Your Center Business for Productive Development

To make long haul business productivity, an organization should put resources into and fortify its center business. We see organizations shrink and bite the dust since they neglect to do exactly that.

The greatest mix-up that organizations make is they attempt to grow excessively far and excessively quick. Of course, development is perfect yet it should be done gradually and in a determined way without forfeiting center business development. Fanning out too quick will destroy basic assets that the center business processes rely upon, in this way debilitating the actual groundwork of your business.

We should investigate how business productivity can be guaranteed by zeroing in on your center business.

Only one out of every odd Open door is Beneficial

Business development systems should zero in on reinforcing the center of a business first. Really at that time should any type of development happen. We see bombed organizations all of the time that did the specific inverse.

Blockbuster is one of the most incredible instances of an organization that moved away from its center shoppers. They would not change their center business to fulfill the need that Netflix capitalized on. The interest began at remote film rentals. Had opportunity and willpower to adjust yet they declined. When Netflix began its advanced web-based features,

Blockbuster had proactively lost the fight.

Another model is Blackberry, which hit its top at 80 million clients. However at that point its opposition begun going to touchscreen innovation. Blackberry disregarded this new innovation and the interest from its target fans, at last losing a portion of the overall industry to its rivals.

Business Development Systems That Work

Here are a few manners by which organizations can accomplish center business development.

1. Streamline your Center Business

Streamlining of center strategic policies implies putting resources into more profound, more grounded procedures. This is the crucial act of business productivity. It's done in various ways, however the most well-known is putting resources into new client obtaining and tracking down inventive ways of conveying your vital items or administrations.

For example, Netflix began as a mail-just membership based film rental help. They saw that their target fans favored the comfort of remaining at home so they dug much more profound into this market by beginning a web-based feature internet, giving their client precisely what they needed - to be engaged in the solace of their homes.

2. Expand the Limits of your Center Business

Development is likewise an essential step for business productivity however the issue is that organizations will quite often extend a lot of at the same time. Take a gander at the business development techniques of organizations like Wal-Shop. They began as only a corporate store and have ventured into regions like basic food item, photography, and, surprisingly, auto. Yet, those extensions didn't occur at the same time. They gradually carried them out over many years.

So organizations ought to extend past their center yet it should be done gradually. The basic principle of thumb is to reinvest 10% to 20% of benefits into expanding the limits of the center business.

3. Reexamine the Business Center

The principal reason organizations like Blockbuster and Blackberry fall flat is they will not reexamine their center business to fulfill new needs Indeed, reexamining a center business is terrible however there are times when it's vital. The capacity to pull this off is typically which isolates winning organizations from those that flame out.

We've seen this like never before with the Coronavirus pandemic. Organizations needed to rehash themselves to address this interesting difficulty. Those that did are as yet flourishing. A large number of them are in an ideal situation now since they found more effective business processes by reexamining their center business or rethought non-center capabilities.

While surveying new open doors, it is critical to decide if it merits the venture and in the event that it takes care of into business benefit. Pose yourself the accompanying inquiries:

Will this new open door reinforce the center of your business?

Might your business at any point turn into a forerunner in this new fragment?

Do you need to take this action as a safeguarding strategy?

Will this open door put your center business in an essential place of life span?

What are the dangers implied with this open door?

Ways Of accomplishing Center Business Benefit

Here are tried and true methodologies utilized by market pioneers to support business benefit through center business development.

Stepping the waters of different socioeconomics to gain new clients for items as well as administrations connected with the center business.

Adding another item or putting in new highlights on current items. Apple Inc. is an excellent illustration of this.

Putting more in promoting to extend the scope and construct

brand mindfulness. This reinforces the center business. Adding more dispersion channels to support reach.

Adding new costs. This moment, we're seeing organizations offer lower section level price tags to get new clients and afterward upselling to those clients.

CHAPTER 10:

CONCLUSION

Organizations should fortify their center system to guarantee business benefit from here on out. Keep in mind, it's not about the present. Fruitful organizations plan ahead too. The cycle ought to constantly focus on fortifying the center business prior to endeavoring to extend. When you are sure that the center business is solid, then, at that point, you can open up new doors.

Promoting is the most invigorating of all business sports. It is the heartbeat of each and every effective business. It is ceaselessly changing in light of the blast of data, the extension of innovation, and the forcefulness of rivalry, at all levels and all over.

All business techniques are advertising systems. Your capacity to think plainly and well about the absolute best showcasing systems, and to ceaselessly change and redesign your exercises, is the way into the fate of your business.

Luckily, similar to all business abilities, promoting can be advanced by training, trial and error, and persistently committing errors.

Also, anything promoting procedure is working for you today, regardless of how

On the planet with more than 70% of web clients dynamic on informal communities, who spend something like one hour daily on normal on those informal organizations, we need to presume that informal communities have turned into a kind of reality where individuals convey, interface, and clearly trust. We additionally must know that more than 60% of those clients access interpersonal organizations by means of cell phones, serious areas of strength for which this percent will just expand later on.

In such a world, we need to concede that interpersonal organizations are another component of reality that has turned into a piece of the business world too. More than 90% advertisers report they are or will involve informal communities for business, while more than 60% of them guarantee to have procured new clients over interpersonal organizations.

The discoveries distributed by business experts and advertisers support the way that organizations can have a ton of advantages from utilizing informal communities, which is the reason execution of those has turned into a piece of business practice. For this reason web-based entertainment promotion is not generally viewed as waiting on the post trial process, however rather it has turned into a

significant piece of the business
world.

9 798871 331644